NATURE'S LUMBERJACK

NATURE'S

by Willis Peterson and Jeffrey Church

with photographs by WILLIS PETERSON

Educational Consultant: LEO FAY, Professor of Education, Indiana University

LUMBERJACK

Follett Publishing Company · Chicago

When Barnaby was born, the beaver dam across the creek was already several years old. His mother and father had watched it and repaired it for two years, and his grandparents had worked on it before that.

In the April that Barnaby was born, all the animals of the beaver colony were busy enlarging their lodge, which stood behind the dam. Four families of beavers lived in the big lodge near the center of the shallow pond, and each family had several new beaver kits, as young beavers are called. Barnaby had two brothers.

Barnaby and his brothers slept on the wood chips that lined the floor of the beaver lodge. They and the other kits stayed in the large room that all the beavers shared. It was about ten feet across and more than three feet high at the middle, so large that even the largest beavers could move about freely.

As the days passed, Barnaby's legs grew stronger. He and the other kits grew restless. Suddenly, they wanted to swim and see the world outside the lodge. They all began to squirm and move around inside the lodge.

For four weeks, Barnaby and his brothers stayed in the lodge. Then one day Barnaby's mother took her family outside, into the water.

At first, the water felt strange and cold to the kits, but soon they started to play. The same day, they learned to float and dive in the clear water of the mountain pond.

They did not really have to learn how to swim, because they were born with an instinct for swimming. But they had to practice swimming to develop their muscles.

The kits were born with many instincts. Many of the important activities of their lives would be guided by instinct.

Because they were beavers, the animals were more at home in water than on land, where they had a funny, clumsy walk. But because they were kits, they even climbed the banks and boxed with one another among the meadow flowers.

Sometimes Barnaby fell over before he was supposed to. His tail was not yet strong enough to steady him while he stood on his back legs.

The young beavers were best at playing among the driftwood and fallen logs of the pond. They learned that their broad, flat tails made loud noises when banged against the surface of the water. Their splashing filled the pond with little waves.

But so much exercise tired them. Then they sat in the sun for hours at a time. The kits did not move, but their quivering noses picked out the spring fragrances of the forest, and their ears caught the delicate woodland sounds.

They heard the rustle of leaves in the wind. They heard musical bird songs. They heard the gnawing sound of the older beavers at work.

So that was how Barnaby spent his first spring weeks—playing with his brothers in the pond.

When spring changed into summer, it was time for Barnaby and the other kits to learn other activities. At first, they had drunk only their mother's milk, but now they were six weeks old, big and strong enough to find their own food. They had watched the old beavers strip bark from trees, and now their mother took the kits with her so they could try it, too.

The family usually left the lodge only at dawn, for it was always cooler in the early morning, or after dark, when fewer enemies of the beavers watched.

Barnaby liked the juicy, tender bark of the aspen tree best. Cottonwood, birch, maple and willow barks were good, too.

Barnaby also learned to help with the daily work of the colony. There were always repairs to be made on the dam, and the lodge was enlarged and repaired constantly.

Of course, the young kits could not do so much work as the older beavers. They would not be fully grown for two years. Now, they weighed only eight pounds; later, their weight might be more than forty pounds. But it was important for them to help all they could; it would be their responsibility to carry on the work when they became adults.

So, gradually, the young beavers developed their special skills. They learned to chisel away the wood around the bottom of a tree. They bit into the wood with their two upper teeth and did the cutting with the sharp lower ones. Their teeth were made perfectly for biting wood.

Barnaby learned to slice through the bark and wood with the first bite, then to make another cut just below it. Then he tore away the wood between the two cuts, and took out a large wedge in the tree trunk. After he had made many cuts in the trunk, the tree fell.

The adult beavers were able to cut down large trees,

but Barnaby and the other young beavers could cut down one of their small saplings in only fifteen minutes.

Once, Barnaby was almost hit by a tree his mother had cut. After that, he always scampered to safety when a cut tree began to creak and groan. All the young kits had to learn to rush away at the sound of a falling tree, for no beaver could make a tree fall in a certain place.

There were other dangers besides being hit. The sound of a tree crashing in the woods could attract enemies. Otters and weasels were especially dangerous to beavers, and young kits were threatened constantly by large owls and hawks.

After the noise of a crashing tree died away, the beavers waited quietly in their hiding places. Then, if no enemy appeared, they hurried back to cut away the branches.

The branches were used to repair and improve the lodge and dam. Work on these projects never stopped. The lodge had to be made larger when families increased, and the dam was made longer when heavy rains washed away the banks. But Barnaby did not really have to learn about the dam and the lodge. Instinct told him that he must help improve them always. They were the most important things in his life, for they were his home and his protection.

One morning, Barnaby was awakened by a commotion. The older beavers rushed from the lodge. The young beavers followed.

Barnaby saw at once what had happened. The level of the water in the underwater passage leading to the lodge had dropped more than a foot.

When he came to the surface of the pond, Barnaby could not see well. He, like all beavers, had poor eyesight, but his keen sense of smell and hearing helped make up for it. He swam toward the dam.

Near one end, a portion of the dam had washed away. The adult beavers were already hard at work. Some brought branches and sticks, and some packed mud and grass around the new wood. However, only the top of the dam had given away.

But a broken dam was a constant danger, so it had to be kept in good repair. It could never be allowed to weaken, for if the water broke through, the beavers would have no pond. Their lodge would stand in a shallow, trickling stream. Several lifetimes of work would be swept away in minutes.

By the middle of the day, the dam was as good as ever. But the beavers had worked hard all along its length. The experience of the morning had been alarming, and all the beavers, young and old, had worked on the dam.

Then some of the older beavers went downstream, below the dam. They began to work in the small stream of water that came through.

Barnaby waddled toward them and discovered that they were gathering mud, stones and short, waterlogged sticks. They were making a framework across the bed of the stream. They were beginning a new dam.

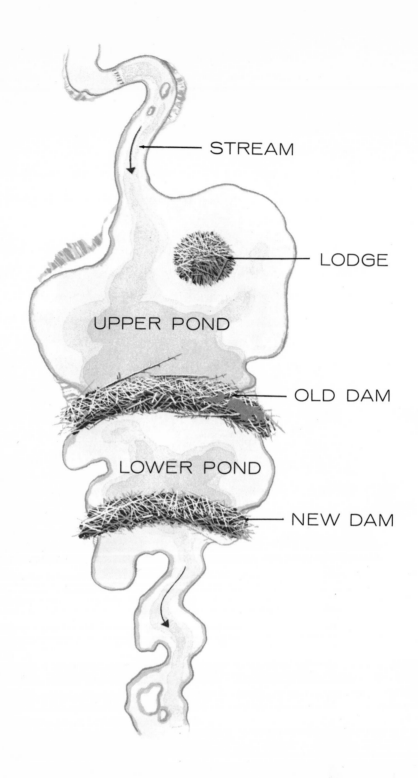

STREAM

LODGE

UPPER POND

OLD DAM

LOWER POND

NEW DAM

Diagram showing how a beaver dam, threatened by a fast stream, was saved. A new dam was built below the old, thus backing up water in front of the original structure.

Barnaby watched. His brothers and some of the other young beavers joined him. They watched the old beavers working. Soon they began gathering small limbs and twigs that would help build a new dam.

It was many weeks before the new structure was large enough to hold back much water. But gradually it grew bigger.

Then a new problem faced the beavers. They had no more wood to build the dam. There was fresh timber upstream, above the old dam, but they could not float it down to the new one. There was also fresh timber downstream, but there was no way to float it up. The stream was too shallow, and the current was against them.

Behind the short, new dam, the water had risen several feet. From there, the older beavers began to dig a trench. Water filled in the trench as soon as they dug it. They dug directly toward a stand of timber about forty yards away.

Barnaby and the others helped all they could. They pawed at the mud and pulled it aside. The old beavers did the hard work, digging the canal deep enough to float the wood they would cut.

In a few days, the canal reached the trees. The older beavers spent many hours deepening and widening it.

When the trench was finished, it was almost two feet wide and deep. The beavers began cutting trees. Now they could float large limbs, and even small trunks, to their new project.

The new dam protected the old dam by making

a pond in front. That meant that there was water pushing on the old structure from both sides. The water behind would have to overcome the push of the water in front before it could wash away the first dam.

Work on the new dam went on through late summer and into the fall. But there was more work to be done. As winter approached, the beavers gathered food to store for winter. When cold weather came to the mountains, the beaver pond would freeze over. Then the beavers would need their stored food. Even though the outside world was shut off by ice, they would have enough to eat.

Barnaby and his brother found tender branches, cut them and dragged them to the pond. They dived with the limbs to the bottom of the pond, where they stuck them into the mud so that they would not come up. If the branches were especially large or tended to float, the beavers held them down with stones from the stream bed.

Winter passed quietly. The beavers had more than enough food stored at the bottom of the pond. It was a cold winter, though, and the water in the pond froze several inches thick.

But time passed quickly, and the ice finally thawed. Spring brought water coursing down the stream bed, and the beaver ponds, behind both the new and old dams, overflowed with clear, cold water.

There was much work to be done on the new dam. It was only half as high as the old one and

not nearly so long. After the heavy flow of water from the spring thaw, the old dam would need repairing, too. Barnaby was not yet an adult, but he could do hard work. He could cut fairly large trees.

One day late in the spring, Barnaby was plastering the top of the lodge with mud. He had just waddled up the little ramp that ran to the roof, when he heard a sound.

He sat upright, his nose quivering, his ears flicking this way and that to catch the sound again. When he heard it once more, he dropped the mud he held in his front paws.

He ran down the ramp quickly and slid into the water. Just as he started his dive for safety, he gave the water a resounding slap with his broad, flat tail to warn the others that there was danger.

As three men rode up on horses, all the beavers made their escape to the water.

The men had equipment with them, and they began unloading it at once. They had several wire cages, which they carried down to the edge of the water. Then they cut several small, tender aspen limbs, trimmed them and placed the branches inside the cages.

The men talked very little as they worked. They finished, mounted their horses and were gone.

Barnaby was one of the first to rise to the surface of the water. He came up cautiously, letting just his nose and eyes break the surface. He swam to the thick weeds near the pond's edge. He waited. There seemed no danger, so he stood up. He sniffed and listened. There was nothing alarming around the pond, so he set about his work again.

Conservation officers ride out in their work of starting new beaver colonies.

A wire cage is set in the midst of tempting branches.

He saw some fine aspen limbs about ten feet away, already cut and trimmed. He swam along the shore line to them. There was also some strange-looking wire in the water that he had never noticed before. He backed away. He sniffed. The wire had a strange smell, but the aspen bark looked so good that he grasped a limb with his forepaws and gave it a yank.

Something clicked. The wire jumped in the water. It banged against Barnaby and knocked him over. He tried to get away, but the wire was

The beaver is caught, unharmed but frightened.

Next the animal is placed in a loosely woven sack, to be carried to its new home.

all around him. He turned in all directions, but everywhere he turned, he found the metal strands of the cage.

Barnaby was caught.

The day passed. Barnaby struggled frantically for a time. Then, tired and frightened, he clung to the wire without moving.

Before morning, the men returned. Barnaby heard them coming and, in a desperate frenzy, made one last effort to escape. By the time the men dismounted and walked toward the pond, he was so exhausted he could not move.

One of the men walked over to Barnaby's cage, pulled it from the water, carried it over near the horses and put it on the ground. Another of the men soon came up with a second cage. He put it down next to Barnaby's. In it was one of the older beavers from the lodge. Before long, there were several cages, and in each one was a beaver from Barnaby's lodge.

Set free, the beaver will soon set about building a new dam.

Then the men got out some sacks. They lifted the beavers from the cages and dropped them head first into the bags.

The men were taking the beavers somewhere on the horses. Barnaby and the other beavers squirmed uncomfortably in the sacks.

After several hours, Barnaby felt the sack being lifted and lowered to the ground. There were sounds outside the sack, and suddenly it was opened. Strong hands grasped Barnaby and picked him up.

He was carried to the edge of a stream, and then he felt cool water come up around his feet.

As soon as he was certain he was free, Barnaby darted toward a pile of thick-leaved branches which the men had cut and placed at the edge of the stream near him. Some of the other beavers had already hidden there and more followed.

The men folded their sacks, mounted their horses and rode away. When they had been gone for some time, Barnaby slipped quietly out of the pile of limbs.

He stood up, bracing himself with his tail. He nibbled at the bark of the branches. The men had left his favorite food, aspen. The other beavers were hungry, too, and they began to eat.

Then the beavers began to explore the strange, new place.

The stream was very small. There was no large pond, no dam and no lodge. All of these would have to be built.

The beavers found fresh timber all along the stream banks. But away from the little stream, the land seemed dry. There were not so many plants as there had been at home.

The beavers began to fell the smaller trees along the stream banks. These would be good material to use for the new dam.

Though the beavers did not know it, that is why the men had brought them here and left the cut branches. They expected the beavers to build a dam here in the mountains that would help make the land fertile.

Here, as in many other places, the water ran away so quickly, down toward the valley, that it did not soak into the soil.

The beavers began their dam by laying mud, stones, waterlogged sticks and plant roots across the bed of the stream. They weighted all this down with stones.

After the foundation was made, the beavers began to place larger material on it. They gathered large sticks, and they cut poles and driftwood into pieces from two to six feet long. They laid these closely together, side by side, on the face of the foundation that was downstream. They placed the sticks in the same direction that the water flowed, so they would not be swept away easily.

The foundation of the dam curved; the middle of the dam was more upstream than the edges. Men build their dams that way, too, for it makes the construction stronger.

Several days went by. After the foundation and the first sticks and poles were in place, the beavers made the whole dam stronger with mud, stones, water plants and grasses.

Next the beavers added larger sticks and pieces of wood, interlacing and strengthening them, until the structure began to emerge from the rapidly rising water.

Finally, they began adding branches gnawed off at various lengths. These were laid on the upstream face of the dam.

The water was already beginning to back up behind it. All the beavers worked together to make a new pond home for themselves.

But water still flowed through the dam in many tiny streams, and the busy animals plastered the new structure with mud and entwining grasses. The stream helped, too. It brought fallen leaves and other debris that lodged against the dam and helped to strengthen it.

In time, plants would grow on top of the dam and send their roots down through it. This, too, would make it stronger.

Before the dam was finished, some of the beavers began to work on the foundation of the lodge. First, they made a little island right in the middle of the stream bed. It was in the center of the pond made by the dam.

They used the same materials they had used to make the dam foundation, but now it was much easier to keep the twigs and stones in place, because the dam had already slowed the current of the stream.

On the little island they had made, the beavers formed a crude circle of sticks and brush. When it was finished, the lodge would stand about three feet high.

The beavers formed several passageways leading underneath to the water by gnawing and adjusting the sticks of the foundation. Then they began work on the walls and roof. For these they used stones, branches and small logs. They interlaced and reinforced the branches.

Soon, the sides and top of the lodge covered the beavers.

Now they were ready to plaster the lodge from the outside. Time after time they grabbed up large loads of mud, leaves and grass, and, waddling up the mud incline they had built, dumped their plaster on the roof.

Busily, they patted and packed the mud in place with their noses and paws.

Before long, the lodge had reached its final, rough form. Of course, the beavers' lodge and their dam would never be completely finished. Barnaby and the other beavers would work on them for as long as they lived.

Spring passed, and summer. That fall, Barnaby helped gather food again. There was fresh timber, and the beavers spent a comfortable winter in their new lodge. The fresh wood chips made the lodge smell new and clean. There was snow in the mountains, and ice covered the stream and pond. But inside the well-built lodge, the beaver families were warm and dry.

At last, the snow began to melt, and when spring arrived, the grass around the new beaver pond came up greener than it had the year before. The

LODGE (in winter)

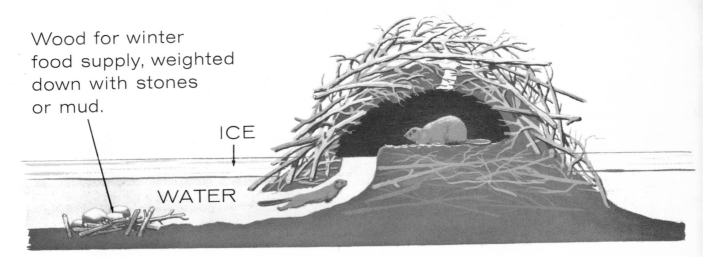

Wood for winter food supply, weighted down with stones or mud.

ICE

WATER

water nourished the land around it and made it produce a rich crop of new plants and grass. Ranchers and farmers who lived on the land near by would be helped by Barnaby's dam.

Baraby was an adult beaver now, and he weighed more than forty pounds.

Early one morning, as he sat on top of the dam, Barnaby heard men approaching. He slipped quickly into the water and splatted it with his large flat tail. There were splashes everywhere as the other beavers swam for safety.

But the men had not come to catch the beavers again. They had come back to see what Barnaby and the other beavers had done for the stream, which had been almost dry when the animals first came to the area.

Now there was a large reservoir of water. The beavers had done their job well.

There would be room for fish in the new body of water. Waterfowl could use the new pond for feeding and as a safe stopover on their long, migratory flights. The land would become more fertile because of the water the beavers had stored to nourish it.

The men were satisfied. They stayed only a short time, and then they were gone.

When Barnaby came up from the water, he peeked cautiously above the surface and found that the shore was empty. Quietly and carefully, he slipped onto the bank and let the warm sun penetrate his fur. The danger had passed. Barnaby was at home in his own pond.

Sometimes men come to fish in the pond that Barnaby and the other beavers made. The dam has grown larger and stronger. Eventually, many of the young beavers will leave this colony and make new lodges for themselves and their families. Then there will be other ponds to nourish the land.

But Barnaby will not go, for this is his home. He has helped build it, and he will grow old here.

THE BEAVER

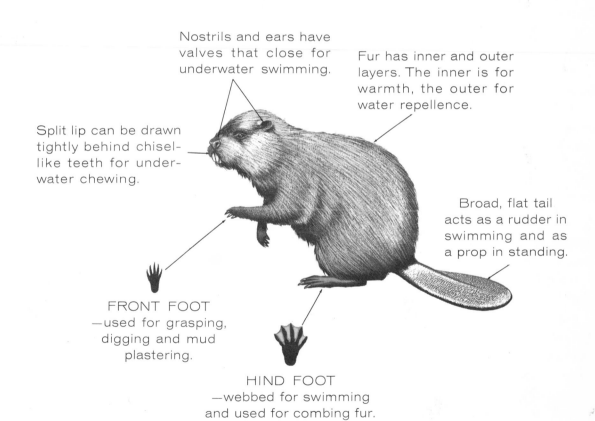

Nostrils and ears have valves that close for underwater swimming.

Fur has inner and outer layers. The inner is for warmth, the outer for water repellence.

Split lip can be drawn tightly behind chisel-like teeth for underwater chewing.

Broad, flat tail acts as a rudder in swimming and as a prop in standing.

FRONT FOOT
—used for grasping, digging and mud plastering.

HIND FOOT
—webbed for swimming and used for combing fur.

GLOSSARY

Key to Pronunciation of Vowels:

a	pat, lap	ėr	her, learn	oi	boil, choice	ə represents any vowel in
ā	ate, tale	i	lid, pit	ou	our, mouse	an unaccented syllable:
ã	bare, stair	ī	mine, kite	u	cut, supper	a in along, e in broken,
ä	car, father	o	cot, hop	ū	use, few	i in pencil, o in melon,
e	red, step	ō	tone, blow	ù	put, wool	u in suppose
ē	sleep, me	ô	border, fall	ü	rule, school	

A heavy mark (′) follows the most strongly accented or stressed syllable in a word (ban′ish); a lighter mark (′) follows a syllable on which there is some stress, usually in a word of many syllables (par tis′ə pa′shən).

chisel (chiz′əl), to cut or shape with a sharp-edged tool.

colony (kol′əni), many animals of the same kind living together.

course (kôrs), to move rapidly; to race, as blood through the veins.

debris (də brē′), rubbish; scattered fragments; ruins.

downstream (doun′strēm′), with the current or flow of a stream.

driftwood (drift′wùd′), wood drifting on or floated by water.

flick (flik), a light, snapping stroke or blow, as with a whip.

forepaws (fôr′pôz′), the front feet of a four-footed animal having claws, as the lion, dog or cat.

foundation (foun dā′shən), the support or base on which something rests.

framework (frām′wėrk′), the structure or skeleton of something; the stiff part which gives something its shape.

frantic (fran′tik), very much excited.

frenzy (fren′zi), great excitement or fury, close to madness.

huddle (hud′əl), to crowd or press close together as if confused or afraid.

incline (in′klīn), a slope or slant.

instinct (in′stingkt), a natural inward impulse that leads a person or animal to behave in a certain way; it is by instinct that animals migrate, fear fire, build nests and train their young.

interlace (in′tər lās′), to unite by or as if by lacing or weaving together.

migratory (mī′grə tô′ri), moving regularly from one place to another, as for food.

muscle (mus′əl), a bundle of tissue in the body which moves a particular part of the body.

nourish (nėr′ish), to supply with food; to feed.

plaster (plas′tər), to cover or smear with or as if with plaster, as on walls and ceilings.

ramp (ramp), a sloping passage or roadway leading up and down.

reinforce (rē′in fôrs′), to strengthen with new force, assistance, material or support.

reservoir (rez′ər vwär), a place where water is collected and kept for future use.

sapling (sap′ling), a young tree.

scamper (skam′pər), to run or move lightly and quickly.

splat (splat), to strike the surface of water with something flat so as to make a loud noise.

trench (trench), a long, narrow ditch.

upstream (up′strēm′), at or toward the source of a stream.

waterfowl (wô′tər foul′), a bird that spends its time at or near water; a swimming bird.

waterlogged (wô′tər lôgd′), so filled or soaked with water as to be heavy and hard to manage, like a log.

wedge (wej), a piece of wood or metal with a thin edge, used to split wood or rocks or to lift a weight.

Grateful credit is given to *Arizona Highways*, its editor, Raymond Carlson, and its staff for their assistance in producing *Nature's Lumberjack*, and to *Friend's Magazine* for permission to use the color plates for the photographs on pages 18, 20, 21 and 28; to Willis Peterson whose photographs appear throughout the book and on the covers; to Jack Stuler for the photograph on page 25; to Tom Culver for the drawings on pages 12, 27 and 31; and to Gene Jarvis for the title-page drawing on pages 2 and 3.